# RACIAL JUSTICE IN AMERICA
## AAPI HISTORIES
# SOUTHEAST ASIAN REFUGEE RESETTLEMENT in the U.S.

## VIRGINIA LOH-HAGAN

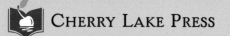
# CHERRY LAKE PRESS

Published in the United States of America by Cherry Lake Publishing Group
Ann Arbor, Michigan
www.cherrylakepublishing.com

Reading Adviser: Beth Walker Gambro, MS, Ed., Reading Consultant, Yorkville, IL
Book Design and Cover Art: Felicia Macheske

Photo Credits: U.S. Central Intelligence Agency via Wikimedia, 5; U.S. National Archives, American Red Cross. Boston Metropolitan Chapter, Identifier: 117700080, 7; U.S. National Archives, Department of Defense. American Forces Information Service , Identifier: 6403448, 9; © mark reinstein/Shutterstock, 11; Library of Congress, Photo by Warren K. Leffler and Thomas J. O'Halloran, LOC Control No: 13; U.S. National Archives, President (1974-1977:Ford). White House Photographic Office, Identifier: 7839930, 14; Photo by Brad Barnes, CC BY 3.0 <https://creativecommons.org/licenses/by/3.0>, via Wikimedia Commons, 17; Official United States Marine Corps Photo No: 1W16-196-2-71 (L) by Sgt. Gregg Sloat via Wikimedia, 19; U.S. National Archives,Department of Defense. Department of the Navy. U.S. Marine Corps. , Identifier: 26398225, 26398269, 26398241, 20; © Andrey Bayda/Shutterstock, 23; © nik wheeler/Alamy Stock Photo, 25; © Jana Shea/Shutterstock, 27

Graphics Throughout: © debra hughes/Shutterstock

**Cherry Lake Press** is an imprint of Cherry Lake Publishing Group.

Library of Congress Cataloging-in-Publication Data

Names: Loh-Hagan, Virginia, author.
Title: Southeast Asian refugee resettlement in the U.S. / by Virginia
   Loh-Hagan.
Other titles: Southeast Asian refugee resettlement in the United States
Description: Ann Arbor, Michigan : Cherry Lake Publishing, 2022.
   | Series: Racial justice in America : AAPI histories | Includes bibliographical
   references and index. | Audience: Grades 4-6
Identifiers: LCCN 2022005318 | ISBN 9781668910924 (paperback)
   | ISBN 9781668909324 (hardcover) | ISBN 9781668914106 (pdf)
   | ISBN 9781668912515 (ebook)
Subjects: LCSH: Indochinese—United States—History—Juvenile literature. |
   Political refugees—United States—Juvenile literature. | Political
   refugees—Indochina—Juvenile literature.
Classification: LCC E184.I43 L64 2022 | DDC 325/210973—dc23/eng/20220214
LC record available at https://lccn.loc.gov/2022005318

Cherry Lake Publishing Group would like to acknowledge the work of the Partnership for 21st Century Learning, a Network of Battelle for Kids. Please visit *http://www.battelleforkids.org/networks/p21* for more information.

Printed in the United States of America

**Dr. Virginia Loh-Hagan** is an author, former K-8 teacher, curriculum designer, and university professor. She's currently the Director of the Asian Pacific Islander Desi American (APIDA) Center at San Diego State University. She is also the Co-Executive Director of the Asian American Education Project. She identifies as Chinese American and is committed to amplifying APIDA communities.

# CHAPTER 1

# Who Are Southeast Asian Refugees?

Imagine waking up to the sounds of war. Your life is in danger. You're no longer safe in your country and need to escape. You flee with only the clothes you're wearing. You're sent to a new country and forced to learn a new language and culture. You're a refugee.

Refugees are displaced people. They're forced to leave their countries. They're escaping war, persecution, or natural disasters. Some are targeted because of who they are or what they believe. Their human rights may have been violated. Refugees leave behind their homes, jobs, and loved ones. They cross international borders. Leaving is the only way they can be safe.

There are close to 30 million refugees around the world. More than 2.7 million Southeast Asian refugees live in the United States. This makes Southeast Asian refugees the largest refugee community in the nation. Many Southeast Asian refugees escaped from the Vietnam War. They identify as Vietnamese, Laotian, Cambodian, Hmong, and others.

Southeast Asia is composed of 11 countries between the Indian and Pacific Oceans.

Sharing global responsibility for refugee issues is the right thing to do. The 1951 Refugee Convention provided international guidelines for helping refugees. It defined who is a refugee. It also defined the rights of refugees. It champions the idea that refugees have a right to international protection. Refugees get legal protection and support. Yet countries have their own laws about immigrants and refugees.

People who are forced to leave their homes have two options. One option is to flee to an area within their home country. In this case, people are known as internally displaced persons (IDPs). Another option is to flee to another country. Crossing international borders makes them refugees. Those who travel directly to another country to seek safety are asylum seekers. They have to prove they're in danger. Seeking asylum is a human right. Everyone should be allowed to enter another country to seek asylum. The second group of refugees flee to another country and wait to relocate to a third country. They're called refugees for resettlement.

**Think About It!** Many refugees take English language classes. They have to learn English to be successful in the United States. Why is this? How would your life be different if you didn't know English?

# DID YOU KNOW...?

At the end of 2020, more than 54 million people were internally displaced. Like refugees, internally displaced people are forced to flee their homes for safety. Unlike refugees, they don't cross international borders. They're not protected by international law. They seek safety wherever they can find it. More than 13 million people are internally displaced in Asia. They're forced to flee because of tropical storms, earthquakes, and political conflicts. People in the United States have been internally displaced as well. In 2005, Hurricane Katrina destroyed much of New Orleans, Louisiana. Around 1.5 million people were forced to leave their homes. About 40 percent couldn't return. They had to make new lives in new places.

# CHAPTER 2

# What Is the History of Refugee Immigration Laws?

The United States has a complicated history with immigration. It tends to favor White immigrants and exclude people of color. This changed with the Immigration and Nationality Act of 1965. This act was the first time the United States accepted immigrants of all nationalities on a roughly equal basis. There was a huge increase in the immigration of skilled workers. Immigrants from the China, Japan, Hong Kong, and India flooded in. These immigrants tended to be more educated and were from middle-class families. They experienced success in the United States. This led to their perception as the "model minority." This stereotype was used to diminish other racial groups.

The refugees who came in the 1970s had a different experience. Mainland Southeast Asia refers to the countries of Cambodia, Laos, Myanmar, Thailand, Vietnam, and Malaysia. In the past, under French colonial rule, this area was called Indochina. A series of wars were fought in this area from 1946 to 1991. Many people fled to seek safety. By 1975, roughly 2 million refugees relocated to the United States.

After the 1965 Immigration Act, immigration jumped to nearly 500,000 people annually, with only 20 percent coming from Europe.

The United States was slow in developing a refugee policy. After World War II (1939–1945), Congress passed the Displaced Persons Act of 1948. This law admitted European refugees.

In the 1970s, the United States was forced to confront the Southeast Asian refugee crisis. In 1975, President Gerald Ford signed the Indochina Migration and Refugee Assistance Act. This law defined Vietnamese, Cambodian, Laotian, and Hmong people as refugees. It gave them permission to come to the United States.

Five years later, President Jimmy Carter signed the 1980 Refugee Act. This law broadened the definition of refugees. Refugees were defined as people with a "well-founded fear of persecution." This act opened the door for more refugees. It also created the Federal Refugee Resettlement Program. This program provided funding and resources to support refugees living in the United States. U.S. Representative Peter Rodino called this law "one of the most important pieces of humanitarian legislation ever enacted by a U.S. Congress."

**Think About It!** Refugees are reviewed by government officials. They have to pass security and medical checks. What are the pros and cons of doing this?

# DID YOU KNOW...?

Many American soldiers serving in the Vietnam War (1954-1975) fathered children there. Born to an American parent, these children were called "Amerasians." In 1971, Representative Patsy Mink fought to pass laws allowing them to enter the United States. Her law was rejected. But in 1982, Congress passed the Amerasian Immigration Act. This law allowed these children to immigrate to the United States. There were several restrictions. But the law did acknowledge "the rightful claim of Amerasian children to American citizenship." These new immigrants received refugee benefits. Because of this law, about 75,000 Amerasians and their family members immigrated to the United States. Only a few hundred stayed in Vietnam.

# CHAPTER 3

# What Was the Vietnam War?

At one time, Vietnam was a country divided. North Vietnam had a communist government. It had allies in South Vietnam, known as the Viet Cong. North Vietnam and the Viet Cong fought against South Vietnam. South Vietnam's main ally was the United States. This war lasted more than 30 years, from 1954 to 1975. It was the longest war in modern history.

North Vietnam had defeated French colonial rule in 1954. It wanted to unify Vietnam under communist rule. Fighting spilled into surrounding countries. The Vietnam War marked the beginning of the war era in mainland Southeast Asia. Fearing the spread of communism, the United States entered the Vietnam War in 1965.

On April 30, 1975, the Vietnam War ended. This event was known as the "fall of Saigon." Today, the former South Vietnam capital city of Saigon is called Ho Chi Minh City. South Vietnam forces were overpowered by North Vietnam. Without U.S. help, they were defeated. Due to its major role in the war, the U.S. government helped evacuate its Southeast Asian allies.

**Think About It!** Americans call the war "The Vietnam War." The North Vietnamese call it the "War Against the Americans to Save the Nation." What does it mean to see the war from different perspectives?

Many Americans were opposed to the Vietnam War. Protests began on college campuses and grew into massive anti-war marches and movements.

# DID YOU KNOW...?

Operation Babylift was the mass evacuation of South Vietnamese orphans in April 1975. These orphans had lost their parents in the Vietnam War. They were brought to the United States and other countries for adoption. The United States put more than 3,000 orphans on planes. Not everyone agreed with this operation. Some thought the orphans weren't necessarily better off in the United States. In 2000, some of the orphans organized Operation Reunite. This program uses DNA testing to find the adoptees' Vietnamese families.

The Vietnam War led to a large population of Vietnamese refugees in the United States. The mass migration of Vietnamese refugees included two separate waves. The first wave of Vietnamese refugees were asylum seekers. They were mostly educated, rich professionals. They included U.S. military employees and South Vietnamese government workers. Their families were able to flee with them. The United States airlifted this first wave.

The next wave were Vietnamese refugees for resettlement. They were known as "boat people." They came from rural areas and were often poor and less educated. They were not evacuated by the United States because of limited resources and space. To flee, they filled boats beyond capacity. They endured many hardships and dangers staying in temporary refugee camps in other Southeast Asian countries, such as Thailand, Malaysia, and the Philippines. Many eventually made it to the United States. But many died at sea.

By 1980, most Vietnamese refugees lived in Southern California. As of 2021, 1.4 million Vietnamese immigrants live in the United States. They are one of the largest Southeast Asian immigrant groups in the country.

# CHAPTER 4

# What Was the Experience of Southeast Asian Refugees?

The **Khmer Rouge** ruled Cambodia from 1975 to 1979. Pol Pot was its leader. He led Cambodia's communist movement. His group killed nearly 500,000 people. The group also displaced roughly 3 million people, close to half of the country's population.

Cambodian refugees immigrated to the United States in three waves. The first wave was just before the Khmer Rouge took over. These refugees joined the Vietnamese who were evacuated by the United States. They were educated and skilled workers. Most were connected to the U.S. or South Vietnamese government.

The second wave was during the Khmer Rouge's rule. These refugees escaped to Thailand. They stayed in refugee camps. They came to the United States around 1978.

The third wave was after the Khmer Rouge was **overthrown**. These refugees were not able to escape in time. They were mostly from rural towns. They stayed at crowded refugee camps with limited resources for long periods of time. They lived in poor conditions. Many immigrated with the passing of the 1980 Refugee Act.

The Khmer Rouge's victims were buried in mass graves like this one.

During this time, Laos was engaged in the Laotian Civil War. Due to the Geneva Conference of 1962, Laos was declared to be neutral. This meant the United States could not openly fight against the North Vietnamese invasion of southern Laos. So the United States launched a secret war in Laos. It wanted to stop the spread of communism in Southeast Asia. It also wanted to cut off supply lines into Vietnam.

The United States bombed Laos from 1964 to 1973. Their secret war became known as the "largest air war." Laos became the world's most heavily bombed nation. The U.S. bombing raids caused widespread devastation. Many people were killed, wounded, and left homeless. By 1975, one-tenth of the Laotian population was dead. Laotians today are still dying from this war. About 30 percent of the dropped bombs failed to explode. More than 20,000 people have been killed or injured by the bombs left behind.

About 25 percent of Laotians were refugees because of the war. Most Laotians fled to neighboring countries. They stayed in refugee camps before relocating to Western countries.

# DID YOU KNOW...?

**SEARAC** stands for the Southeast Asia Resource Action Center. It is a national civil rights organization. It empowers Cambodian, Laotian, and Vietnamese American communities. It stands together with other refugee communities, people of color, and social justice movements to fight for equity. It was founded in 1979 as the Indochina Refugee Action Center. It was formed by a group of Americans concerned about what was happening in Southeast Asia. It pushed the United States to welcome and protect Southeast Asian refugees. Its efforts led to the passage of the Refugee Act of 1980 and the creation of the Office of Refugee Resettlement.

Many Southeast Asians who fought alongside the U.S. military were in danger from the new communist governments and needed asylum.

One group affected by the Laotian Civil War were the Hmong. The Hmong are an ethnic minority who live in the rural highlands of Laos and its surrounding areas.

The United States recruited and trained thousands of Hmong people to fight against communist Vietnamese forces in Laos. The Hmong soldiers sacrificed much to help the United States. The United States felt it needed to provide asylum to the surviving Hmong soldiers and their families. These Hmong refugees arrived in the United States in the late 1970s.

Similar to other refugees, the Hmong were scattered in different cities in the United States. This was not ideal for Hmong clan culture. Some Hmong chose to remain in Thai refugee camps. They hoped to return to their homelands in Laos. Over time, Thai refugee camps closed down. Hmong refugees realized they wouldn't be able to safely return to Laos. This led to an increase in Hmong immigration to the United States.

**Think About It!** Hmong and Laotian veterans that served for the United States during the Vietnam War received American citizenship. What do you think about this?

# CHAPTER 5

# What Was Resettlement Like?

The United States had specific resettlement policies. When refugees arrived, they were spread out into various cities and states. They were scattered throughout the country. There were two main reasons for this. First, the United States wanted to encourage assimilation. The goal was to have refugees fit into American society as quickly as possible. This included learning English and American cultural ways.

The second reason for spreading out refugees was to not overburden a few cities. The United States wanted to distribute the economic impact. Refugees required a lot of resources and supports. However, they also contributed to the workforce and increased the economy. It seemed fair to place refugees in different places.

Many refugees were sent to places that were very different from their homelands. For example, many Hmong were sent to live in Minnesota. Minnesota is very different from the hills of Laos. It's cold and snowy. As former farmers, the Hmong had to learn a different way to live. Hmong refugees built strong communities both in Minnesota and central California.

Texas, Washington, New York, and California have resettled the most refugees.

 **Think About It!** Southeast Asian refugees were displaced and relocated several times. They struggled to form a sense of home and belonging. What would it be like to be a refugee? What challenges do you think they face?

The refugees were mainly relocated to poor areas of cities. At first, they felt isolated and were in shock. But once settled, some refugees moved to or formed ethnic enclaves. Many refugees created thriving communities. Community leaders built businesses and neighborhoods. They helped one another and fought for their rights. They also created safe spaces to speak their languages and practice their traditions.

Life was not easy for the Southeast Asian refugees. Some were not welcomed. They were detained by police and treated like criminals. Some had a hard time settling. They faced poverty and racism. Many Americans resented or feared the refugees. They saw them as foreigners and thought they were taking away their resources. The truth is that refugees pay taxes and increase the economy just like all Americans.

In addition to facing language and cultural barriers, refugees also dealt with trauma. As war refugees, they lived with violence. They suffered from depression. Cambodian refugees have the highest level of mental health distress of all the Southeast Asian refugees. Many Southeast Asian refugees don't trust the government. This makes it hard to ask for help and seek care.

Many Cambodians settled in Long Beach, California. There they created a "Cambodia Town."

# DID YOU KNOW...?

In the 1970s, Vietnamese refugees settled in Seadrift, Texas. They became crab and shrimp fishermen and were doing well. White fishermen accused the refugees of taking away their jobs. They formed White mobs and set the refugees' boats on fire. In 1979, a fight broke out between the Vietnamese and White fishermen. A White man was killed. The white supremacy group Ku Klux Klan (KKK) hosted rallies against the refugees. They bullied and harassed them. Once again, the refugees fled for safety. Eventually, they fought back by taking the KKK to court. Today, some Vietnamese refugees have returned to Seadrift and formed a thriving community.

# CHAPTER 6

# What Is Happening Today?

Until recently, the United States had admitted more refugees than all other nations combined. But this changed under President Donald Trump. Trump reduced the number of refugees allowed to immigrate. He also increased security checks, which prolonged the time it took to process refugees. Meanwhile, refugees were left in dangerous situations for very long periods.

In 2021, the United States withdrew its armed forces from Afghanistan. This created a refugee crisis. Many Afghan people were forced to flee. Afghans fought for spots on U.S. military flights out of Afghanistan. This brought back memories for many Vietnamese refugees. Vietnamese refugees have reached out to help the Afghan people. They have donated money. They have provided housing and legal help. They have called U.S. officials to let in as many Afghan refugees as possible.

Bee Nguyen is a politician. She was the first Vietnamese American elected to the Georgia House of Representatives. She said, "The reality is in Vietnam and Afghanistan, the United States played a role in what happened. And, part of our responsibility is to acknowledge that role and to open up our country to the people who have been impacted by it."

As a world power, the United States has a responsibility to help others. Our refugee policies should reflect our commitment to humanity.

Many Southeast Asian American communities in the United States are still facing challenges. Because of where Southeast Asian refugees were placed, many youths grew up in poor neighborhoods with failing schools. This resulted in poor educational outcomes. Some young people dropped out of school. Some turned to crime, gangs, and drugs for survival. They felt like they didn't have any options due to racism and poverty.

Today, Southeast Asian refugees are three times more likely to be deported because of old criminal convictions. Many of these refugees are currently living lawful lives. They are being punished for mistakes made in the past.

Many of those deported were born in refugee camps. They have never stepped foot in their native countries. In 2017, more than 200 Cambodian and Vietnamese refugees were rounded up for deportation. Many were lawful permanent residents. Southeast Asian American activists are fighting for the rights of these refugees to stay with their families.

Also, thousands of refugees have not been fully processed. Without final deportation orders, they moved on and rebuilt their lives. But they could be deported at any time. This results in a lot of stress. Despite many hardships, Southeast Asian refugees have survived and thrived.

**Think About It!** In 2020, the United States settled only 11,814 refugees. This is the fewest in any year since the U.S. refugee program started. What are the reasons for this? Do you think we should admit more or fewer refugees?

# DID YOU KNOW...?

Many Southeast Asian refugees were born in refugee camps. This fact makes them hard to deport. Where would they go? They're not citizens of their native country. They also aren't citizens of the countries hosting refugee camps. They are "stateless." Being born stateless is challenging. People need nationality documentation to access resources. For example, many stateless people are denied medical care and education. They also have a hard time finding jobs. In addition, they lack safety, security, and a sense of belonging. Laws determine nationality. Many activists are pushing for reforms that prevent people from being stateless.

# SHOW WHAT YOU KNOW!

Major injustices happened as a result of the Vietnam War. The war created a refugee crisis. Refugees needed a place to settle. They also needed support to resettle. There are still refugees today. Let's work to welcome and support refugees.

The histories and stories of Southeast Asian immigrants are invisible or incomplete. Often, students learn about the Vietnam War and the refugees from a White American viewpoint. Learn more about the Southeast Asian refugee experience.

Show what you know! Choose one or more of these activities:

- Visit communities of Southeast Asian refugees. Eat their foods. Learn more about their cultures.

- Interview a Southeast Asian refugee or read biographies about Southeast Asian refugees. Learn about their struggles and successes.

- Compare the Southeast Asian refugees to Asian immigrants who came as a result of the 1965 Immigration Act. Examine how and why they are different.

- Read all the books in the *Racial Justice in America* series. Create a journal, podcast, or social media campaign. Include a segment about Southeast Asian refugees.

 **Think About It!** Think about all the things you have learned. What would you like to learn more about?

# SHOW WHAT YOU CAN DO!

Share your learning. Being an ally is the first step in racial justice work. Allies recognize their privilege. We all come from different positions of privilege. We also have different types of privilege. In the United States, being White is a privilege. Other examples include being male or an English speaker.

Use your privileges. Use it to help all achieve equality. Learning about Southeast Asian refugees taught us that refugees have a unique experience. Unlike other immigrants, they fled for safety. Governments decided where they would go. Refugees need support. Here are ways you can be an ally:

- Volunteer to teach refugees English.

- Fight for laws and programs that support refugees.

- Share how refugees have benefited the nation.

We all have a role to play in racial injustice. We also have a role in making a better world. Do your part. Commit to racial justice!

**Think About It!** Think about your privileges. Do you want to improve the lives of others? What are you willing to give up to do this?

## EXTEND YOUR LEARNING

### NONFICTION

Gottschall, Meghan. *Xin Chào, Vietnam*. Ann Arbor, MI: Cherry Lake Publishing, 2021.

Loh-Hagan, Virginia. *A is for Asian American: An Asian Pacific Islander Desi American Alphabet Book*. Ann Arbor, MI: Sleeping Bear Press, 2022.

O'Connor, Jim. *What Was the Vietnam War?* New York, NY: Penguin Workshop, 2019.

Rouse, Victorya. *Finding Refuge: Real-Life Immigration Stories from Young People*. Minneapolis, MN: Zest Books, 2021.

Public Broadcasting Service: Asian Americans
*https://www.pbs.org/weta/asian-americans*

## GLOSSARY

**airlifted** (AYR-lift-uhd) moved people, troops, or goods by air, especially in a war or when routes are closed

**ally** (AH-lye) a person or group that provides assistance and support in an ongoing effort, activity, or struggle

**assimilation** (uh-sih-muh-LAY-shuhn) absorption of individuals or groups of differing ethnic heritage into the dominant culture of a society

**asylum** (uh-SY-luhm) a place that offers safety

**colonial** (kuh-LOH-nee-uhl) relating to being controlled or governed by another nation

**communist** (KAHM-yuh-nist) a type of government where all property is owned by the government and profits are shared by all

**convention** (kuhn-VEN-shuhn) a formal meeting or gathering where people discuss shared interests

**deported** (dih-PORT-uhd) sent a person back to their country of birth

**ethnic enclaves** (ETH-nik EN-klayvs) communities or areas that include many people from the same culture or ethnic background

**evacuate** (ih-VAH-kyuh-wayt) to move or take away from a dangerous place

**Hmong** (MUHNG) an ethnic group of Southeast Asia

**humanitarian** (HYOO-mah-nuh-TEHR-ee-uhn) related to improving the lives and living conditions of other people

**human rights** (HYOO-muhn RYTS) rights belonging to all people

**Khmer Rouge** (kuh-MEER ROOZH) members of a violent communist political party that took control over Cambodia

**migration** (my-GRAY-shuhn) the movement of people or animals from one area to another

**native** (NAY-tiv) having origin in a country or area

**neutral** (NOO-truhl) not taking any side in an argument or contest

**overthrown** (oh-vuhr-THROHN) removed from power

**permanent residents** (PUHR-muh-nuhnt REH-zuh-duhntz) people who have the legal right to live and work in a country

**persecution** (puhr-suh-KYOO-shuhn) mistreatment or abuse

**poverty** (PAH-vuhr-tee) the state of not having enough money for basic needs such as food, water, or shelter

**privilege** (PRIV-lij) a special, unearned right or advantage given to a chosen person or group

**racism** (RAY-sih-zuhm) treating people unfairly because of their skin color or background

**trauma** (TRAH-muh) an emotional response to a terrible event

**violated** (VYE-uh-lay-tuhd) broken or disregarded

## INDEX